Sad But O.K.

My Daddy died Today

A Child's View of Death

Barbara Frisbie Juneau

D1522286

Blue Dolphin Publishing
1988

Published by Blue Dolphin Publishing, Inc.
P.O. Box 1908, Nevada City, CA 95959

ISBN: 0-931892-19-8

Library of Congress Catalog Number:

Juneau, Barbara Frisbie, 1944-
      Sad but O.K. : my daddy died today : a child's view of
death / by Barbara Frisbie Juneau.
           p.   cm.
      Summary: Through the eyes of her nine-year-old
daughter, the author shares the events that befell her
family during the time the author's husband was faced
with a terminal brain tumor.
      ISBN 0-931892-19-8 : $9.95
      1. Children and death—Juvenile literature. 2. Terminally
ill—Family relationships—Juvenile literature. 3. Brain—
Tumors—Patients—Family relationships—Juvenile
literature. [1. Death. 2. Cancer—Patients.] I. Title
BF723.D3J85 1988
155.9'37—dc19

Printed in the United States of America by
Blue Dolphin Press, Inc., Grass Valley, California

9 8 7 6 5 4 3 2 1

Dedication

**Lovingly dedicated to a pair
of very special mothers—
Margaret Garriott
and Kay Frisbie**

Contents

The Airport
1

A Visit to the Hospital
13

The Last Christmas
26

Help with Projects
33

A Trip to the Snow
40

Projects and Parties
48

A Few Last Outings
54

A Visit to the Cemetery
60

The Funeral Service
72

Epilogue
81

A Note From The Author

Suddenly, death was headed straight for my family and there didn't seem to be anything we could do to stop it. We had dodged it, sidestepped it, postponed it, and finally, reluctantly recognized its inevitability.

In November of 1977, my husband Dennis had undergone surgery for the removal of a brain tumor. Unfortunately, most of the tumor could not be disturbed without causing damage. And so, during the ensuing months, he had undergone both radiation and chemotherapy treatments. There was hope at first, however the treatments proved to be powerless in halting the rapidly growing tumor.

How do you tell your children that their father is dying? It is not an easy task. I tried to be honest with them from the beginning. I prayed for the right words to use, and I hounded the book stores for books dealing with death and dying.

There were several good books for adults and a few which were aimed at children, but most of these centered on the child's feelings and actions

AFTER a death in the family. What of the thoughts and feelings of the children who must watch the life of a loved one slowly slip away? Should we shelter them from reality and maintain a sense of false hope? I don't believe that is the answer. Our children deserve more.

Through the eyes of my nine-year-old daughter, Kelly, I have attempted to share the thoughts and feelings of one family faced with impending death. The way we handled a terminal illness may not work for everyone, but if it helps even one family, the time has been well spent.

About The "Author"

At the time of her father's death, Kelly was nine years old. The following was written by her in September 1978, as a 5th-grade assignment on a "special experience."

MY EXPERIENCE

My name is Kelly, I am 10 years old. I have 2 younger sisters: Their names are Karin and Katie. They are 7 and 2 years old.

Just this last year we had a very scary and sad experience in our home. My dad had been having bad headaches for a couple months, and finally went to the hospital.

The doctor said that he had a brain tumor. He stayed in the hospital for about 3 weeks and had surgery on November 3rd. After his surgery he was recovering quickly and went back to work for about 3 weeks but then he started getting worse.

We had a fun time on our trip to the snow in February. We made snowmen and had a great time.

When we got back from our trip, my dad started getting even worse. On the last 2 or 3 days before his death, he couldn't eat. On the night before his death he got pneumonia, and the doctor didn't think he would live through the night. The next day he was in a coma and finally died. That was a very sad experience for me, because I thought he was the best dad in the world.

Sad, But O.K.

My Daddy Died Today

A Child's View of Death

The Airport

"Is Daddy on that one?" Karin asked every time a plane flew over.

"Don't be silly," I answered. That's not even a jet!" Sometimes little sisters could be so dumb.

"Girls, don't get too far ahead of me," Mom called. Then she picked up my youngest sister Katie, who had been stopping every few feet to examine something on the ground, and headed toward us.

My sisters and I had just finished an early dinner in the airport cafe. Mom and Dad would be eating later at a church potluck. We had almost a half hour to wait before my father's plane arrived. So as we walked toward the United Airlines terminal, there was plenty of time to pause and watch the planes come and go. After a while the cold October wind forced us to go inside to the terminal waiting room. Here we waited anxiously for the announced arrival of Dad's plane. Katie, only one and a half, passed the time by climbing on and off all the chairs. Occasionally she would stop by a window. Then she would press her face against the glass to try to get a better look at the planes outside. Once in a while she would climb up on Mom's lap for a quick hug.

"Flight Number 107 from Los Angeles will be arriving in five minutes," announced the loud speaker.

"It's about time," I remarked as Mom grabbed Karin and Katie by the hand and we all rushed outside to watch for the plane. At first we could barely see it. It was only a speck in the cloudy sky. Gradually it grew larger and larger and then it touched down effortlessly at the end of the runway. The engines roared as the big jet struggled to a stop. Then the plane made a wide sweeping turn and headed right at us.

The airport in Santa Barbara is quite small. The Spanish-style building never seems to have enough room for the waiting passengers, and the tails of the larger jets can be seen above the roof of the terminal building from the parking area. People waiting outside become totally surrounded by the sight, sound and smell of the jets. CAUTION - JET FUMES reads a sign on the four foot brick wall which separates waiting passengers and friends from the plane's "parking place."

As the plane got closer, Katie held her ears because the noise of the jet scared her. Mom lifted her up so she could see the steps being wheeled into position. Karin watched anxiously for Dad. I remembered that Dad had gone on trips before and was never one of the first to get off. Today, however, he seemed to be taking longer than usual.

"There he is!" shouted Karin. Unable to control her excitement, her brown hair blew wildly in the wind as she jumped up and down.

I saw him too. "Why is he walking so funny?" I asked turning toward Mom. Then I noticed a worried expression creep over her face and I felt a little bit scared.

"He's probably tired from all the travel," Mom answered without taking her eyes off him.

We watched helplessly from behind the gate as Dad shuffled slowly toward us. His arms were overflowing with a briefcase, overcoat, umbrella and extra papers that didn't fit in his case. When he finally entered the waiting area, I tried to help by taking some of his things.

"Don't touch anything! I finally got everything all arranged after dropping them all day long." His voice was harsh and almost angry, but yet he was smiling.

"Is Dad drunk or something?" I whispered to my mom.

"Just hush. Let's go," she said as she kissed Dad on the cheek.

"Can I carry your umbrella?" Karin shrieked.

"No!" he snapped. Then in a softer voice said, "It's okay, I can manage."

Mom took his arm and steadied him as we walked toward the baggage area. A couple of times Dad lost his balance and almost fell. Mom guided us to a nearby bench to sit for a minute. Once he was off his feet we were able to take Dad's overcoat and umbrella from his lap.

"The luggage won't be out for a little while yet. Why don't I take you and the girls to the car," Mom suggested. "Then I'll come back and get your things. I know you're tired, and besides Katie is getting out of hand."

Once he was safely in the van resting on the back seat, Mom hurried back toward the baggage area leaving me in charge of things. I didn't know why Dad was acting so strangely, but I could sense that Mom was very concerned. I knew that he had been having a lot of headaches during the past month. 'Could a headache bother someone's walking?' I wondered to myself. No, I didn't think so. Maybe he was just tired from his trip.

Dad had left a few days ago for some interviews in Poughkeepsie, New York. He worked for IBM Corporation and the family had talked about moving lots of times. In fact, friends used to joke about IBM standing for I've Been Moved. It seemed that IBM employees were always being moved around the country and now our family was planning a move from California to New York.

The move would probably take place before Thanksgiving. A college student had been hired to paint the outside of the house and the last few weeks had been spent getting the inside of the house ready to put up for sale. Turning a four-bedroom split-level house that definitely looked "lived in" into a home that had a place for everything with everything in its place was not an easy task.

I had mixed feelings about moving away from Santa Barbara. It had been my only home. I thought to myself, 'I'll miss all my friends . . . but I do want to live where it snows. I like my house . . . but maybe I'll get a bigger bedroom in my new house.' I guess I was more eager to move than to stay.

"What's Poughkeepsie like?" I asked turning toward Dad.

"When are we moving?" interrupted Karin.

"Oh probably in a few weeks, I guess. We may even have a white Christmas this year," he answered. Then he described the area around Poughkeepsie, comparing it in climate and geography to

5

Brookfield, Connecticut where we had visited the previous summer. There would be lots of trees and green hills, with rivers and lakes nearby. I thought it sounded pretty nice.

Soon Mom returned with the baggage and after paying the parking lot attendant, we began the short ten-minute drive home.

"I think I'd better call the doctor as soon as I can," Mom said, glancing over her shoulder at Dad who was lying on the back seat of the van.

"I'm okay. Really I am. I guess I just need to get some rest," he muttered, shielding his eyes from the glare of the setting sun. Suddenly he rolled onto the floor as the van turned a corner. I was scared!

"Hold on!" Karin yelled as we helped Dad back onto the seat. Katie thought it was funny.

"Daddy fall down," she giggled.

At home it took both Mom and me to help him up the stairs. At last he flopped onto the queen-sized bed and lay there peacefully half-asleep.

I sat on the foot of the bed while my mom dialed the phone impatiently. She hoped the doctor was still in his office even though a glance toward the clock showed it was already 5:30.

"Yes, I know the office is closed, but Dr. Halling often stays late. Would you please ring his office for me?" She was insistent but calm. It seemed like forever before she spoke again. I was worried because I could tell that she was worried.

"Yes, thank you." She paused briefly. "Dr. Halling, I just picked Dennis up from the airport

6

and he is having trouble walking. I think maybe he should go to the hospital for tests." Her voice started to tremble, "Okay, fine. I'll meet you there as soon as possible."

Dad had seen Dr. Halling before his trip about the headaches which seemed to be getting worse. Maybe when they got him to the hospital they would finally be able to find out what was causing them.

Mom looked at Dad momentarily as he lay dozing on the bed. Then she headed down the stairs calling over her shoulder, "Kelly, I'll be right back. Keep an eye on Katie for a minute." Bang! The door shut and she was gone. After a few minutes she was back with the girl next door. "Brenda will stay with you girls while I take Dad to see the doctor. We'll be back as soon as we can."

Her voice was in a hurry, but she had to move slowly as she helped Dad downstairs and outside to the station wagon. It would be easier to park than the van. Almost as an afterthought she turned and yelled, "Be good." I could see that tears were trickling down her cheeks and suddenly my own eyes were full of tears too.

Several hours later Mom came back alone. "The doctor wants to do a lot of tests to find out what's causing Dad's headaches. He may have to stay in the hospital for a few days." Then she made a series of short phone calls. I didn't hear everything she said, but what I did hear made it clear to me that Mom was very concerned.

"Hi Grandma. Listen, I don't want to upset you, but I thought you'd want to know that Dennis is in the hospital for some tests. No, you don't need to come down. I'll keep you informed. Give our love to Grandpa."

"Hello Gordy, this is Barbara. I just wanted to let you know that Den made it back from New York, but he's still having pretty bad headaches and the doctor wants to do some tests. I'm sure he'll be wanting to talk to you about the interviews as soon as he's feeling better. He'll be in the hospital at least through Monday, so you might want to drop by and talk to him." Gordy was Dad's boss at IBM.

"Pastor, listen, don't wait for us to start eating. I just left Den at the hospital for some tests. His headaches seemed to have gotten worse while he was away. Tell everyone I'll be in touch as soon as we know anything." Mom and Dad would not make it to the potluck dinner with the church choir tonight.

"You'd better get to bed now Kelly," Mom said as she hung up the phone. Since I was nine and the oldest, I had been allowed to stay up a little longer than my sisters. Karin and Katie had both been tucked into bed about a half-hour earlier.

"Okay Mom ... but," I said hesitating, "do you know what's the matter with Dad?"

"No honey, I don't. But it's probably just some type of infection. He's been running a slight fever this past week. Now hurry along to bed and don't

8

forget to say your prayers," she said as she kissed me goodnight. It had been a busy day.

Reluctantly I went to bed, but it was not easy for me to get to sleep. Over and over in my mind I wondered, 'What could be wrong with my dad?' Finally, exhausted, I drifted off to sleep.

The next morning Katie was sitting in her high chair munching dry Cheerios when Karin and I wandered into the kitchen half-asleep. We were surprised to find Mrs. Lemkuil fixing breakfast for us.

"Where's Mom?" Karin asked between yawns.

"She left for the hospital about a half-hour ago, but she'll be back soon. And until she's back, 'Auntie Ruth' will be here with you." She wasn't really our aunt, just a good friend from church that loved little kids, especially babies.

Mom made several trips to the hospital that day and someone was always home babysitting Katie while she was away. Karin and I played with our friends in the neighborhood just like we did every Saturday. I hoped Dad would be home soon. All my friends kept asking about when I was going to be moving and I didn't know what to tell them.

On Sunday, Mom made arrangements for us to get to Sunday School and Church and she spent the morning at the hospital. Later she met the rest of us at some friends' home for Sunday dinner. Ron and Janet Crabb had planned the dinner earlier in the week and they were anxious to hear all about Poughkeepsie and the upcoming move.

"Den brought home all kinds of information on housing, churches and schools. He was really very impressed with the area. We should hear something next week on exactly which position he will have," Mom explained as she and Janet worked in the kitchen.

"Is dessert ready yet?" I asked.

"Just a couple more minutes," replied Janet. Then she turned back to her conversation with Mom. "We really don't want you to go, you know?" she continued as she dished up dessert.

"I know, but just think of us as a good excuse for visiting the east coast," Mom joked. "You know we'll always keep in touch. Your family is too important to us to let a few thousand miles come between our friendship."

The adults took their dessert to the living room and continued to talk about the fun times our families had had over the years. All of us kids played outside and nothing more was said about how Dad was doing. It was probably the first time since Friday afternoon that life seemed almost normal for me.

Soon however, we were home again with a babysitter while Mom made another visit to the hospital.

Karin ran to the window when she heard the car pull into the driveway later that evening. "It's Mom, and Aunt Judy's here too!" she giggled as she bolted toward the door. "Hi Mom. Hi Judy," she said with outstretched arms waiting for Judy to pick her up. Judy was my dad's sister.

"Look who I ran into at the hospital. She's going to stay with us for a few days until Dad comes home."

"Gee, this is just like Christmas," Karin said on Monday when Grandma Frisbie and her sister "Aunt Polly" arrived. Dad hadn't shown even the slightest improvement over the weekend and Grandma had insisted on coming down to help out. It was fun to have all the extra people around, but there was tension in the air and I wanted my dad home too!

Monday was Halloween. Aunt Polly and Judy helped us get into our costumes while Mom and Grandma were at the hospital. Karin and I went trick-or-treating around the neighborhood with our friends while Katie was the official door-opener at home. "I get IT!" she would screech at the sound of the doorbell. And anyone who got between her and the door had better watch out. She probably had as much fun passing out candy as we had collecting it.

Karin and I were still up when Mom and Grandma came through the door. And, Grandpa Frisbie was here now too. He had flown in from a business trip about an hour earlier and now lay exhausted on the living room floor.

"Did you have a good time girls?" Mom smiled. Then, without waiting for an answer, she continued,

"Well, get along to bed now. It's late, and after all there is school tomorrow."

Reluctantly we kissed everyone good night and moved slowly up the stairs counting candy as we went.

"I'll trade you a Baby Ruth for a Sugar Daddy," Karin pleaded as we headed toward our rooms.

A Visit to the Hospital

MOM HAD ALREADY LEFT for the hospital the next morning when we woke up. However, she was at home in the kitchen when we rushed into the house after school that afternoon.

"Hi girls. Did you have a nice day?" she called when she heard the door open.

"Hi Mom. School was okay, I guess," I answered while I looked for something to eat. I was starved. "How's Dad today?"

"When's he coming home?" Karin quizzed eagerly.

"Not for a while I'm afraid," Mom replied while pulling out a kitchen chair. "While you're eating your snack, I'll try to bring you up to date on Dad's condition. The doctor did an x-ray called a CAT Scan on Dad, and he says that Dad has a brain tumor."

"What's a tumor?" we both asked at the same time.

"That's a good question. Dad's tumor is a clump of cells growing in his brain that shouldn't be there. It has been pushing on his brain and

13

causing it to swell and that's why he has been having so many bad headaches. On Thursday the doctors are going to do an operation and try to remove the tumor."

"Will that make Dad well again?" I asked.

"We don't know for sure. We will just have to hope and pray it will." Then she added in a cheerful voice. "Dr. Halling said you girls could all come to the hospital tonight for a visit. How does that sound?"

"I thought kids weren't allowed in hospitals!" I responded.

"Well sometimes they make exceptions when the doctor gives the okay. Besides, Daddy asked him if you could come. We won't be able to stay too long though."

"Oh goody!" chuckled Karin as I nodded a silent okay.

Many friends from our church and neighborhood had begun to bring meals over for us during the past few days. They knew Mom was spending many hours a day at the hospital and really didn't have time to do a lot of cooking. It seemed like we received dinner every night, and friends would also invite me and my sisters over to play so Mom and the other relatives could have some time to themselves. Grandma and Grandpa Frisbie, Judy and Polly would all be staying until after the surgery. I was sorry about my dad being in the hospital, but I did like all the special attention we were getting. The Pastor had even prayed out loud for our family in church last Sunday.

Later that evening as we drove to the hospital, I started to recall the only other time I had been in a hospital room. It was when I was seven years old and Dad had taken me and Karin to see Mom after she'd had a miscarriage. I carefully pictured that day in my mind.

"Go on, give Mommy a kiss, girls," Dad had urged. I was scared to go too close. She had seemed so sick.

"What's that for?" I had asked pointing to a big needle in her arm. It was connected to a bottle hanging above the bed. I remembered that Karin had gone right to Mom's side and hugged her. At four Karin didn't seem bothered by anything. Or maybe she had just been so glad to see Mom that she didn't notice any of the strange stuff in the room.

"It's okay. That's just some liquid food to help me get my strength back."

After I had given Mom a quick hug, I sat down on a chair at the foot of the bed. As we talked, I watched as nurses helped other patients in the room. It was a busy place, and I was glad when it was time to leave.

A hospital is an interesting place, but it can also be very frightening the first time you visit one. I hoped that tonight's visit would go well and that my dad was getting better.

When we arrived at the hospital I was pleasantly surprised. Dad was feeling much better. The nurses had been giving him shots to help the swelling go down. In fact, it didn't really seem to

me like he was sick at all. He even laughed and told some jokes.

We enjoyed the time we spent with Dad that night. He had a private room so only the family was there. Soon he began to tell us all more about his trip and the nice church he had found in Poughkeepsie.

"Are we still going to move?" Karin asked curiously.

"I hope so. Only I guess it won't be as soon as we hoped. We may have to wait until next year for that white Christmas," he said smiling.

We stayed for about half an hour and then Katie started to get restless. She wanted to climb on and off the bed to "hug Daddy again." After a while Grandma took us home so Mom could stay and visit a little longer.

The next day when we came to visit we had lots of surprises for Dad. My Girl Scout Troop and Karin's classroom had made get well cards for him. We both felt very special to have so many friends caring about our dad. Most of the cards just said "Get Well, Mr. Frisbie" and had pictures on them. Others were quite clever, and some were even funny.

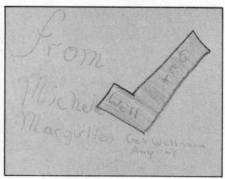

Dad's surgery took about seven hours, so everyone except Aunt Polly was still at the hospital when we got home from school Thursday. Grandma and Judy arrived home at dinner time.

"Well," Judy told us, "the operation is over, but your mom and Grandpa stayed to talk to your dad in the recovery room. They'll be home in about an hour and your mom will tell you all about it."

I was glad the surgery was finally over. Maybe Dad would get to come home soon. I was really beginning to miss him.

Later that evening Mom tried to explain the surgery to Karin and me. "The doctors found a tumor deep inside Dad's brain. They could only get part of it out. Now they will try to destroy the rest of it with some radiation treatments."

"How come they couldn't take it all out?" I asked angrily.

Mom pulled me onto her lap and with a deep sigh continued to speak. "When a tumor is in another part of the body such as the breast or stomach, the surgeon usually removes the whole tumor plus a little extra around it to make sure that no cancer cells have gotten into the area near the tumor where they can start to grow again."

"That's gross!" interrupted Karin.

"In the brain this is impossible. Cutting away any area of the brain is very dangerous because it controls our whole body. A tiny little area regulates our breathing, another controls our various movements, some parts store our memories, and others have to do with our five senses. If the doctor had destroyed any of the important areas of the brain, Dad could have died during the surgery or possibly have been paralyzed or blind when he woke up."

"You mean Dad could have died today?" I asked unbelievably.

"I didn't want to worry you, but yes, brain surgery is very serious." She pulled Karin closer to her side and continued softly. "It's okay, he didn't die. And you know what? The doctor said he'll probably be able to come home in about a week. Isn't that good news?"

"Yeah, great," I mumbled to myself.

The many prayers that the surgery would go well were answered on that day. No one knew how Dad would do in the months ahead, but he was alive and strong today.

The next day when we saw him, he had a big bandage around his head. It looked like a turban. He seemed to be a lot better, although the right side of his face was quite swollen and the puffy eyelid made his one eye no more than a slit. He would have to stay in the hospital about a week longer, but at least his headaches were gone. He was in a different room now and it was full of plants and flowers and an unbelievable number of cards. Karin and I had taken him some more homemade ones too.

Dad was home with us again only eight days after his operation. His bandage had been replaced now with a gauze stocking cap and he had a big rectangular-shaped ink pen drawing on the side of his head.

"Who did that?" Karin asked pointing at the design when she first saw him.

"The radiologist who will be giving me treatments did that. He's a doctor," Dad answered.

"Oh, it looks funny," laughed Karin as she hurried off to play. Karin never hesitated to ask about anything she saw. However, I was a little bit more hesitant to blurt out questions. Later that evening when I was alone with Mom I asked, "What's a radiologist and does Dad really have to have those funny marks on his head?"

"They do look funny I know, but these will help the doctors to kill off the rest of the tumor so it won't start growing again." Then she said that the tumor was found to be malignant or cancerous and. . . .

"You mean Dad has CANCER?" I interrupted loudly. I didn't know very much about tumors, but I knew that cancer was awful!

"Yes, not all tumors are cancerous, but this one just happened to be. And, radiation treatments were started today before we left the hospital. This means that a big x-ray machine is aimed at the tumor to try to kill the rest of it."

"Will it work?" I asked timidly. Suddenly my stomach didn't feel very well.

"We won't know for several weeks, but you mustn't tease Dad about those markings. The machine they use is very powerful and it destroys both good cells and bad. The marks will help the doctors to aim the machine at the right spot each time. We don't want them to miss the tumor, do we?" she asked with a smile.

I shook my head to indicate 'no' and then hurried off to bed. Why was all of this happening to my dad? It wasn't fair! Somehow I drifted off to sleep, convinced that there wasn't anything that I could do about it myself.

The treatments would last several weeks. Meanwhile Dad continued to wear a stocking style cap to keep his head warm. Whenever someone has surgery on their head, all their hair has to be shaved off and it takes a while for it to grow back.

Now Dad had a new doctor who was a cancer specialist, and he had to go for visits fairly often. One time we all went along because Dr. Henderson wanted to meet us and answer any questions Karin and I had about Dad's illness. Katie was too young to understand what was going on so he didn't need to talk to her. Mom had told us that he wanted to talk to us in private while she and Dad waited in another room.

We didn't say much, mostly just listened as we headed down the hall toward another office. The doctor was a big man, maybe seven feet tall, and he had a fuzzy mustache.

"Now which one is Kelly and which one is Karin?" he inquired as he motioned for us to sit down. "I have two daughters, and you know what? Their names both start with a 'K' too." He had a nice smile.

He told us about not being able to remove the whole tumor and that was the reason Dad was having the radiation treatments.

"Do you have any questions?" We both shook our heads silently, then Karin giggled. He told us that we hadn't done anything to cause Dad to get sick and that we couldn't catch the disease from him. He didn't say Dad would die, but he didn't say he would get well either. As a doctor he was going to try everything he could to help Dad get better. I liked him. He was honest and didn't treat us like babies.

He was funny too. "You know what? Your dad's hair is starting to grow back now, but pretty soon it's all going to fall out again," he said while tugging at Karin's hair. This would be because of the powerful x-rays killing off the hair roots. He said we could come back anytime we had questions and he would gladly try to answer them. I thought Dad was lucky to have such a nice doctor.

During the next few weeks things were almost normal at our house. The relatives had gone home and Dad, although still easily tired, was getting along fine. His hair was even growing in and he looked a lot like he did in his wedding pictures when he had a crew cut. People came by to see him at lunch time, and Mom would sometimes drop him by the office to visit his friends. The doctors didn't want him to drive yet because there was still some swelling that was interfering with his side vision.

Before I knew it, we were packing up the camper to head for Grandma and Grandpa's in Saratoga. We always went there for Thanksgiving and they came to our house for Christmas. Mom did the driving and everything went fine until Katie had a "mommy attack." She was riding in her port-a-crib behind Dad's seat and nothing he did seemed to quiet her down.

"Mommy, Mommy!" she screamed, her little arms reaching desperately towards the driver's seat. Finally Dad couldn't stand it anymore.

"Pull over. I'll drive for a while until you quiet her down."

"Kelly, come play with her a little bit," Mom called to me, and then turning to Dad said, "You know you're not suppose to drive until the doctor gives you the okay."

"I'm all right. I'll be very careful and it will just be until you get her to sleep. I just can't stand that screeching—it's giving me a headache."

23

"Okay," Mom said reluctantly as she headed up the next off-ramp so they could switch places.

Karin and I glanced at each other and hopped up onto the upper bed. We were worried that Dad couldn't see well and it was almost dark. We watched carefully to make sure he stayed in his lane. Bump! Bump! Bump! The raised lane markers rumbled as our tires crossed over them.

"What are we doing?" I called to Mom, my voice trembling as I spoke.

"Shh. We're just passing a slow car," she answered quietly as she rocked Katie slowly back and forth, never taking her eyes off the road ahead.

"Dear God, please help my daddy to drive good and not let us get in an accident," prayed Karin, and after a while I realized that we would be safe. Pretty soon Katie was sleeping soundly in her crib, and Mom and Dad talked quietly.

"See, I told you I could drive all right."

"I know, just following the doctor's orders." She smiled and patted his hand gently.

After about an hour had passed, Mom resumed the driver's seat and before we knew it we were pulling into Grandma's driveway. "How was your trip?" Grandpa asked as he started to unload our things.

"Pretty good," said Dad eagerly, "I even drove a little bit."

It was quite late so we were ushered off to bed after a little snack. In the morning I would get to help cut up bread and celery for the stuffing. It felt good to know that I was big enough to help with the dinner this year.

Once the turkey was in the oven, there wasn't much to do but wait. The adults were content to watch one football game after another, and Karin and I played some games until Mom made us put them away.

"Kelly always wins," cried Karin.

"Why does Karin always have to be first?" I added.

"If you can't play nicely, put the things away," Mom said.

I think that's Mom's favorite expression. Karin and I frowned at each other and then took Katie outside for a walk. Dinner would be ready soon.

When we gathered at the table, Dad started to read a Bible story from his devotional booklet about the ten lepers who were cleansed and how only one of the ten had returned to thank God for healing him. Before he finished the last few lines, he was fighting back tears. I don't think I had ever seen my dad cry before, and my eyes watered too.

Mom took the booklet, finished the story and asked the blessing on the food and also thanked God for our safe trip and Dad's speedy recovery from the surgery. It had been three weeks ago today since the operation and he was almost his old self again. His hair was getting longer too!

The Last Christmas

ON DECEMBER 5TH Dad returned to work at IBM. His friends were all glad to see him doing so well and welcomed his return. One morning when I came upstairs to say good bye before leaving for school, he stood smiling at himself in the bedroom mirror.

"I just can't get this fuzzy stuff to lie flat," he said in my direction while he brushed his hair toward one side. "Another week or so and I should have it under control."

He still went for radiation treatments every day, and within the week his hair started falling out in big patches all over his head. I could tell that it bothered him. Only a few days earlier he had felt and looked almost normal, but Dr. Henderson had been right, soon he would be bald again.

Christmas was just around the corner and we hadn't taken any pictures for our cards this year. It had been a tradition to send picture cards since my first Christmas in 1968. Rather than break tradition, Mom and Dad decided to use a family picture that had been taken at our church the previous May. There were many of our friends who did not know about Dad's illness so they composed the following letter to enclose in our cards this year:

CHRISTMAS 1977

Dear Friends and Relatives,

Our picture this year is not the typical one you would expect to find inside—it was taken at our church last May. However, the year 1977 has not been a typical year for our family. It has been a year of many blessings, but it has also brought trials and sufferings.

First let me say that one of our blessings this year was a six-week vacation to the East coast. During this time of travel we were able to visit many relatives and friends whom we hadn't seen in several years. It was an educational trip for us all as we witnessed life in various parts of the country from as far south as Georgia and north to Massachusetts. It was also a time that brought a special closeness to our family. Driving 9000 miles and living out of a camper for six weeks has a special way of uniting a family and fosters a spirit of greater cooperation and shared responsibilities. We believe that this special time of togetherness was granted to us in preparation for the time when we would all share the burden of a trial.

For those of you who are unaware of the happenings of the last few months, I will attempt to bring you up to date.

We had originally planned to send out a family picture taken in front of our NEW HOME somewhere in Poughkeepsie, New York. In October, we thought it would be only a matter of weeks before we would be transferred and settled in a new town 3000 miles away. We were busy preparing our house for sale—painting and yard work had been completed by the weekend of October 23rd. Den left for his interviews on Tuesday and it was with a spirit of great excitement that the girls and I anticipated his return on Friday. Things had gone well in Poughkeepsie. Despite almost constant headaches, Den had undergone four interviews, found a new church and met with the pastor, investigated schools and housing, and generally scrutinized the area.

When he stepped off the airplane, shock is the only word capable of describing my reaction to what I saw. My excitement was gone. Den appeared almost to be in a trance. The combination of headaches, lack of sleep and all day travel had taken its toll. I realized that only God's protection could have brought him safely home.

It was only a matter of about 45 minutes before we arrived at the hospital. Our doctor met us there and agreed that observation and tests would be necessary to find the cause of the headaches. He was admitted and although I sensed a real seriousness to the situation, it was not until Monday evening that we were first confronted with the phrase that still sticks in my throat—brain tumor.

Surgery was performed on November 3rd and we praise the Lord for Den's rapid recovery. He was released on the 11th. Unfortunately the surgeon could not safely remove the entire tumor and radiation treatments have been necessary. Aside from hair loss, Den has had no side effects from the treatments and he is back to his normal routine and activities. He returned to work on December 5th and we daily give thanks to God for the care He has given us during these times.

We are especially thankful to our many friends and relatives who have shared their time to provide companionship, babysitters and meals for us. Also for the many prayers which have been offered on our behalf by all of you.

We will not be moving to New York. However we are not ruling out the possibility of a transfer to Boulder, Colorado. A lot will depend on future tests which will indicate the effectiveness of the radiation treatments. At this time we are very encouraged by Den's progress. He has been bowling and golfing and will soon be singing in our choir's performance of the Messiah. There has been no recurrence of headaches whatsoever.

Only the Lord knows what the future holds for us. We are without fear or worry in this situation because we trust in Him alone to bring us through. We would ask that you continue to remember us in your thoughts and prayers.

May each and every one of you have a truly Blessed Christmas.

With love,

Dennis, Barbara, Kelly, Karin and Katie

We had a terrific Christmas. Dad was doing great and we had a lot of fun Christmas shopping with him. He always took Karin and me out to buy Mom some surprises. Then we would make a big deal out of bringing in the gifts and telling her to be sure and stay out of the room where we were wrapping them. Often we would wrap up silly things or something very practical that we wanted her to have. It was fun to have a lot of gifts under the tree.

I remembered last year when Mom wanted an electric broom, Dad took a child's play broom and attached an electric cord to it and wrapped it up.

"What's this?" she had giggled as she lifted it from the box.

"Well, you said you wanted an electric broom," Dad answered very seriously before we all broke out in uproarious laughter. A few minutes later he brought a real one in from the garage.

Christmas day in 1977 came on a Sunday. Naturally I was afraid we would not possibly have time to open all our gifts before church services. We were not allowed to get up before 7 o'clock, and with Grandma, Grandpa and Aunt Judy there it always seemed to take about three hours to complete passing out the gifts and opening them. We had a family tradition of opening one gift at a time as we went around the room from youngest to oldest.

"Do we have to go to church tomorrow?" I asked timidly before kissing Dad good night. I was afraid I already knew the answer.

"We are going to church even if we have to stop when YOU are right in the middle of unwrapping a present," he said before his smiling face took on a more sober expression. "After all, you haven't forgotten whose birthday we will be celebrating tomorrow, have you?"

"No," I mumbled. "C'mon Karin, the sooner we get to sleep the faster tomorrow will come. Good night everybody."

Our morning was filled with joy, laughter and thanksgiving. We arrived at church services with time to spare. "Joy to the World, the Lord has come," rang out the congregation as we gathered together to worship on this very special day.

"I wonder if Mana will be waiting for us at home?" Karin said as we pulled out of the parking lot.

"Probably," I answered.

"I wonder what she brought us," she said, her eyes as big as saucers.

"Probably nothing," I kidded. She knew Mana usually gave us anything we asked for. She was Mom's mother and enjoyed spoiling us. She and her friend Joe, as well as Uncle Ronnie who was home on leave from the army, were waiting in front of the house when we pulled up. They usually came up from Los Angeles to join us for Christmas dinner.

Dad had an especially nice Christmas and as usual we took lots of movies and pictures. This would be our last Christmas together as a family, although I didn't realize it at the time—Dad seemed to be improving with each passing day.

Help with Projects

MOM AND DAD HAD started several projects around the house to keep everyone busy. One of them was converting part of the garage into a laundry-sewing room. Grandpa and Dad did most of the framing and putting up of the wallboard, although Mom and Judy helped too.

Grandpa and Grandma would have to go home soon, but they were waiting to hear the results of Dad's new brain scan made the day after Christmas.

They use a machine called a "CAT SCAN" to take computerized x-rays of the brain or other parts of the body. Tumors are very easily seen on these pictures and by doing this the doctors would be able to tell if the tumor had gotten any smaller since the surgery.

One night after my grandparents had left, I overheard Mom talking on the phone to a friend.

"No new tumors have sprung up anywhere and there was some indication that portions in the center of the tumor have been destroyed."

That sounded good to me. And afterall, Dad looked and felt so good. True, he had started a second series of radiation treatments, but what did that matter. They weren't painful and he couldn't possibly lose any more hair—he was completely bald now.

On New Year's Day Dad went out to the laundry room between football games to do some work.

"What'cha doing Dad?" I asked as I sat on a nearby stool to watch.

"Thought I'd work on the lighting out here so we can see what we're doing." He stood on a chair and started to screw the fluorescent light fixture to the ceiling.

"C'mon now. What's the matter?" he mumbled. I looked up to see his hand tremble every time he started to turn the screwdriver. After a few minutes he threw the tool to the floor and went back into the house. I followed him inside and watched as he turned up the TV and plopped down onto the couch.

"Den, Ron and Dave are here to see you," Mom called to him as two of Dad's closest friends appeared in the doorway.

"Now that the Rose Bowl game is over, I thought Dave and I would come by and help you get that wiring finished up," Ron said.

"Great! I worked on it earlier myself, but my silly hand just wouldn't cooperate with me." Dad tried to cover his frustration with a joke as he sprung up from his seat.

The lights were all in working order within a couple of hours. Many good friends would come to the rescue during the coming months.

A few days later Dad began to have occasional headaches again, and although he seemed perfectly normal most of the time, he would suddenly have spells of weakness in the left side of his body.

"Why does he lean that way when he walks?" I asked Mom one day.

"He can't help it!" chimed Karin defensively.

"That's right girls. He can't help it. The tumor was on the right side of his brain and that is where the control of the left side of the body is located. We can be grateful that in a right-handed person the speech and thought centers are on the left side. The doctor said if Dad started to have any trouble from the tumor that it would probably be with his left side. He may have weak spells from time to time, and we will just have to try to be there when he needs help."

"He can hold on to me whenever he needs to," Karin stated proudly.

"That's fine, honey. I'm sure Daddy will appreciate your help."

I didn't understand. I wanted my dad to be his old self again—laughing and swinging me over his shoulder like I was a mere sack of potatoes. We hadn't been able to wrestle with him on Saturday mornings in a long time. Karin and I loved this time every week when we would gang up on him in bed. Of course he would let us win the match until he'd had enough. Then, all of a sudden his big hands would come out of nowhere holding us both motionless until we cried, "OK! OK! That's enough. We'll go out now!"

The minute he let go we would both run to the safety of the hallway before chanting, "Ha Ha! Can't get me now." I missed that old Dad.

One of the things he enjoyed doing most was putting together slide shows with music for special IBM meetings. These were very elaborate productions involving six projectors, three ten-foot screens and slides automatically coordinated to music and narration. He and George, a co-worker, had been doing at least one show a year for as long as I could remember. Last spring they had done a real nice one for a manager's conference. The theme was "200 Years of Work in America." Unfortunately, Mom had sorted through all the slides and removed our personal ones back in September when we were getting ready to move. There was a big meeting coming up on January 11th in Glendale and Dad and George wanted to get the slides back together for one last showing.

"Don't touch anything please," Dad cautioned as I leaned over the large piece of plexiglass balanced delicately on a large cardboard carton. A bare light bulb shown brightly from below illuminating hundreds of slides.

"Did you take that picture?" Karin pointed to a slide of the Statue of Liberty, accidentally knocking several slides to the floor.

"You girls better go outside for a while and play. You can see the show when it's all ready to go," Mom warned from the doorway as she entered carrying two cups of coffee.

She liked helping them with the slides and usually had some good suggestions for their arrangement. She worked especially hard this time because she felt badly about messing them up in the first place.

"Sorry guys, but I really didn't think you would be using this again," I heard her say as we left the room. I always enjoyed it when they came to our house and had slides lying out all over the place. We were probably the only kids who ever got to see these special shows.

The closer the meeting came the worse Dad seemed to get. He was having occasional trouble with his left leg and foot now, sometimes stumbling or falling, but the problems often went away as quickly as they came.

A few nights before the meeting, Dad went out to the garage to start gathering up the screens and equipment they would be needing.

"George of the Jungle's here," giggled Karin as she stood in the doorway waiting for him to bring something in from his car.

Suddenly Mom yelled from the garage, "Kelly, tell George to come out here right away!"

"Why, what's wrong?"

"Just call George!"

By the time we got to the garage, Mom was helping Dad up from the floor. "Are you Okay?" she said softly, her eyes focused directly into his.

"Yeah. It was the strangest thing. All of a sudden my leg just collapsed and I said to myself— I'm gonna fall over and there's nothing I can do to stop it. Seems sturdy enough now," he said applying his weight to his left foot.

Later that evening Dad called his boss and asked if it would be all right for Mom to go along and help set up for the meeting. They went down the next afternoon and spent the night because it was an early morning breakfast meeting and it would take several hours to set things up.

Before they left, I was helping Mom load things into the van and noticed pools of tears glistening in her eyes. "What's the matter? Is Daddy worse?"

"No, " she paused, "Not yet." A few tears escaped and rolled slowly down her face.

"Not yet," I echoed angrily as I headed toward my room jumping every other step as I went. Why did MY DAD have to get sick!

Janet Crabb came over to stay with us while my parents were gone, and the meeting turned out pretty well. While they were unloading the car the next day I heard Dad say, "Well George, I'd say that was a pretty good 'swan song' for the team of Ritter and Frisbie, wouldn't you" George nodded in agreement. It was the last show they ever did.

Karin and I were back into all our regular activities now that the holidays were over. We belonged to a Pioneer Girls group at a nearby church and Karin reported that her group prayed for Dad regularly. I was too shy to mention his illness in my own group, but I prayed for him when I was alone and my Sunday School class at our own church always mentioned him in their prayers.

One Wednesday night after Pioneer Girls Karin asked Mom, "How come Daddy isn't getting any better when we are all praying so much for him?"

Mom hesitated.

"Do you think God is too busy answering other people's prayers who maybe prayed before us—and when He's done He will help our daddy?"

"I don't know, honey. Sometimes God doesn't answer our prayers the way we would like Him to. We just have to keep on praying and God will answer us in His own time and His own way."

Now even Karin had noticed that Dad was getting worse.

A Trip to the Snow

BY THE END OF JANUARY, Dad had to stop driving again. He was having trouble with his vision on the left side and had scraped a car while pulling into a parking space one day. He still went to work, but Gordy would usually stop by and pick him up in the morning, and when he went out to call on customers he went with John Karolus. John had been his co-worker and one of his best friends for more than ten years.

This driving arrangement went on for about a week. Then Dad started having trouble walking even short distances without assistance. His problem seemed to be like one of balance, and if he was near a wall, furniture or even another person, he could steady himself. At home Karin and I helped out by keeping an eye on him as he moved about. Unfortunately since our house was a split-level, there were a lot of steps that made it harder for him to get around. He had fallen a couple of times and we didn't like to leave him home alone now in case he needed help getting up. We were glad when Aunt Judy came back again to stay with us.

Finally Mom convinced him to take a week or so off until he was walking a little better. It embarrassed Dad to have to depend on friends at work to help him do something as natural as walking.

February 8th was the annual Pioneer Girls father-daughter banquet. This year it was being held at a local pizza parlor and we were going to ride with Ron and Chrissy Crabb. Dad was starting to get a little bored now that he hadn't worked for a while, so he asked Mom to take him over a little early so he and Ron would have a chance to visit.

"Can't we stay now too?" Karin and I begged as Mom started outside to the car.

"Sure, that will be fine," answered Janet before Mom had a chance to say no.

"But you didn't bring your sweaters."

"You have to bring Dad a jacket. You can bring us our sweaters at the same time. Please, Mom, please?"

A short time later the horn honked and we ran to the car, glad that she had returned so soon. It was a chilly Wednesday evening.

"Let me help you Dad. We're going to be late," I offered.

"It's okay. I'll get it in a minute." He was struggling to zip his jacket while he talked unhurriedly to Ron. Twenty minutes later we were all in the car headed for the banquet.

The noisy chatter of fifty or so girls bounced off the walls. It was hard to hear the person sitting next to you. While we waited for the pizzas we played some Bible games and were amazed at the number of questions we couldn't answer. A few hours later, having had our fill of pizza and noise, we returned home to find Mom waiting anxiously.

"Did you have a good time?"

"Yeah, it was nice. Save these game sheets," said Dad, "we may want to use them at church sometime."

"Sure," Mom answered, helping him off with his jacket before he had a chance to do it himself. Over the past week I had noticed her gradually doing more and more for Dad without asking or being asked.

It had been several weeks since the end of the last radiation series and now that Dad was having problems, Dr. Henderson believed that some chemotherapy might be helpful. This involved being injected with medication through an I.V. one day, and then taking a pill every day for two weeks. Dad had about five days of pills left on Saturday, February 25th when we prepared to head off for a long weekend in the snow at Big Bear.

"Thought maybe you might like a little help," said Janet as they pulled up about a half-hour early. Mom and I were loading things into the camper.

"How'd you know?" Mom uttered, somewhat relieved. "Maybe Ron could load up the ice chest for me; it's pretty heavy."

Although Aunt Judy was still here and would be going with us, the morning had not started out well. When they had helped Dad out of bed, they discovered that the sheets were wet. Dad had wet the bed and didn't even know it! The medicine made him real funny—like he was stuck in slow motion or something.

Aunt Judy had helped him downstairs for breakfast while Mom stripped the bed and started the washer. Unfortunately this was just an indication of the things that lay ahead during the next few days.

We were lucky that not only were Judy and the Crabbs along, but also Lynn Bennett and her two boys. It became more and more obvious as the day wore on that Dad would require a lot of help during the weekend.

"What are you going to have for lunch, Den?" Lynn asked when we stopped at a Bob's Big Boy. He didn't answer. Slowly he looked up from the menu and stared silently into space.

At first we thought he didn't hear the question, but then after a few minutes he began to speak very slowly. He did almost everything in slow motion. Talking, chewing, walking. It was weird.

Nothing went right that day. After going halfway up the mountain, we had to turn around and go up the other side. A mudslide had closed the road the day before. It was well after dark before we located the cabin we were renting.

"Oh boy! Look at the snow," I said opening the door of the van. "Brrr. Where's my jacket?" The temperature must have been somewhere in the twenties.

Mom and Ron trudged around in the snow trying to turn on the water and gas to the cabin. Then we all had to unload the van and carry everything up a hill through ten inches of soft snow.

By the time we finished getting everything situated in the cabin and ate dinner, it was time for bed.

"Get down you guys. Mom, the boys won't leave us alone!" yelled Chrissy Crabb as she hit her brother Steve with a pillow.

"That's enough now you kids. Stay in your own beds."

Karin, Chrissy and I were sleeping in a loft above the kitchen and Steve and the Bennett boys were in the bedroom. They just couldn't resist teasing us as they sneaked up the ladder yelling, "There's a mouse!" Of course they really didn't see any of the furry gray creatures, but we knew there were some nearby. The last sounds I heard that night were those tiny claws scratching busily along the timbers.

When we awoke the next morning the sun was shining brightly on the snow-covered slope that stretched up from behind the cabin. It was going to be a beautiful day for playing in the snow.

We had a ball sliding down the hill on sleds and inner tubes. Occasionally Mom and the other mothers would come outside for a while, and they even took a few turns at sliding down the hill, but I didn't see much of Dad that day.

At dinner time he ate his food very slowly and two people would have to support him when he walked and tell him to move his feet.

I was embarrassed a little because he frequently had trouble getting to the bathroom in time. It didn't seem to bother any of the adults. They all tried to help Dad any way they could. I know he didn't have much fun at the snow. Mostly

he sat in the cabin by the fire and dozed a lot. One day he sat outside in a patio chair and watched us come down the hill on innertubes and snow pans. All the kids had a lot of fun and were disappointed when we left on Monday instead of Tuesday, as had been planned.

"Do we have to go home today?" I pleaded.

"Yes, girls. There is a big storm due to hit here tonight. You don't want to get snowed in, do you?"

"Yeah! That would be neat," hollered all us kids.

Well, as usual, the adults got their way and we began to pack. With Dad so helpless, we had to lug everything down the hill to the van. Naturally Karin and I resented having to make so many trips to the van with our stuff. Sometimes I was angry with God for letting my dad get sick, and this was one of those times. We had been spoiled in the past because Dad had always done most of the loading and now WE were even having to help get HIM to the van.

Once we were home, I learned that the approaching storm was not the only reason for our early departure. Mom was talking to some friends about the weekend and related how difficult it had been on all the adults. It had not been all the physical help that Dad had required which was hardest on them—this they all eagerly gave. Mom said it was actually painful to watch Dad so utterly helpless and, emotionally, they were all drained by the experience. I guess the Bennetts and the Crabbs were the only non-family members who ever fully realized the strain Mom and Judy had been under while caring for Dad on a twenty-four hour basis.

When the next weekend arrived, things had changed considerably. The medication must have gone out of Dad's system because, except for a little unsteadiness, he was back to his normal self again. Maybe he was going to get well after all!

Projects and Parties

ONE OF THE OTHER PROJECTS Mom and Dad had begun recently was some remodeling in our family room. Little by little over the last three years they had worked together putting up cedar shingles and redwood boards to give the room a rustic look. Last year Dad had completed the upper part and now all that remained was the bottom counter with a sink. During the holidays a friend built some cabinets for us and Mom and Judy covered the fronts with redwood and tiled the counter top. Dad helped as much as he could, but he was starting to tire easily now, so he enjoyed lying on the sofa observing the progress. One day Dave Thornton came by to work on the plumbing and Dad insisted on helping.

"Here Dave, I can do that. Hand me the wrench."

They both kind of chuckled in an understanding way as Dad started to work under the sink and then slowly rolled to one side.

"I guess you'd better take over," Dad said to Dave reluctantly.

"Okay, but I need your help. Here, hold this for me," Dave said as he pulled up a bean bag chair and propped Dad up beside him on the floor. Actually, Dad just ended up supervising, but Mr. Thornton had a special way of making him feel useful and involved.

Mom was anxious to have the project finished because Dad wanted to have an open house for his friends from the office. So many people wanted to come to see Dad, but I guess they thought they might be imposing. Mom suggested a short open house for anyone who wanted to drop by to visit, and the idea of a party delighted Dad.

About the time the project was completed, Grandma and Grandpa returned to help with the plans for the open house which was to be held on March 10th.

"Please, Mom, can't I stay here and help?" I pleaded one last time before Karin, Katie and I were ushered off to some friends that night for dinner. I guess Mom thought we'd be in the way, and I guess it was a good thing we left because about 60-70 people were there.

"That was the most fun I've had for a long time," Dad said later that evening.

"I thought so too," Mom echoed his feelings.

I guess some people might think it's silly to have a party when you have cancer, but Dad talked like he really enjoyed himself. I guess it was nice for him to be able to talk with his friends in a cheerful party atmosphere. I bet for a few short hours he was able to almost forget he was sick.

49

On Saturday, we celebrated Katie's 2nd birthday by having several families over for cake and ice cream. Katie was especially excited on this day. She ran around the room playing with balloons and then climbed up in Dad's lap for a while. I wonder if she sensed that something was wrong with him.

"Is Daddy going to get well?" Karin asked a few days later.

"I don't think so, unless God sends a miracle," Mom answered quietly. Then she explained that God does not always answer our prayers in the manner we would like Him to. And, sometimes when a person is very ill, He uses death to end their suffering instead of healing them. Karin started to cry and then Mom and I did too. She hugged us tightly.

"You know girls, we will miss Dad very much when he is gone, but we must remember one very important thing. We still have each other and we will be all right because the same God who is going to end Daddy's pain and take him home is going to be here to take care of us."

"But can't we do ANYTHING?" I pleaded.

Mom replied, "About Dad's health, no. The doctor says the tumor is obviously growing again."

My dad was dying and we couldn't do anything to prevent it. His life was in God's hands.

"The one thing we can do," Mom continued, "is to make his remaining life comfortable and happy."

"How do we do that?" Karin asked between sobs.

"Show him how much you love him by continuing to share the little experiences of your days with him and ask for his help and advice so that he continues to feel needed as a father. The one thing that we should not do is withdraw from his life."

"We won't do that," Karin stated firmly.

Mom also went on to tell us that we can show our love by being considerate when Dad was resting and not bring our friends in and out. Dad felt very strongly about never returning to the hospital since there was nothing that could be done to help him. Therefore he would be at home with us until the very end.

On March 12th Dad's former manager and very close friend, Andy Ploegstra arrived from South Dakota for a visit. He had been transferred there two years ago and we had been fortunate enough to visit them the two previous summers while we were passing through on vacation. Even though we didn't see them as often now, we remained close friends.

Mom says that Andy was the one responsible for encouraging us to attend El Camino Church. For several years prior to us joining the church, we had attended special Christmas Programs at the invitation of Andy. Mom and Dad had not attended church services regularly since they were teenagers, but when Karin and I were little they began to think about joining a church again.

Dad seemed to perk up upon Andy's arrival. Although he stayed with the Thornton's, Andy spent most of his time with Dad. They went places and did things around the house. Dad could still get around pretty well with a little support from one person, however we rented a wheelchair for when distances were far or he was especially tired.

I remember one night Andy and Mom took Dad to see a special talent show that several of our friends from church were involved in.

"Did you have a good time?" I asked him the next morning.

"It was a very funny show, Kelly," he responded, "and I didn't get too tired to enjoy it because I didn't have to walk from the parking lot!"

It had become quite an effort for him to walk more than very short distances, so I guess Dad enjoyed riding in the wheelchair.

While Andy was here we finished the laundry room project. Andy even helped out with the painting. I guess about fifteen people had helped with that room by the time it was completed. I know Dad really pushed himself while Andy was here, because after he left, Dad relaxed and we could see that his condition was getting worse fast.

"Why does Dad seem so quiet all the time?" I asked one night.

"Dad is having very bad headaches again," Mom replied. The look on her face was strained.

A Few Last Outings

MOM AND DAD WERE both determined to live as normal a life as possible, and to them normal meant spending time with their friends.

"It smells good, but it sure looks yucky," Karin said as she watched the pig emerge from the "gunny sack".

It was March 18th and our family was attending a Mexican Pig Roast with people from IBM. Some friends had dug a big pit in their backyard and wrapped the pork in gunny sacks to roast all night.

"It tastes pretty good," Dad said as he took a small bite.

Actually, I liked the salsa, beans and the salad the best. There were kids to play with so I had fun. Dad couldn't do much besides sit in his chair and talk, but he did enjoy the food.

Grandma and Grandpa came back again— they had gone home during Andy's visit so Dad would feel free to spend most of his time with his friend. One day Mom, Dad and my grandparents all went out to the cemetery to look at some sites Mom had selected. It seems that even though Dad did not like to talk much about his worsening condition, he wanted to help Mom as much as possible to handle things ahead of time.

The week before they went, Mom asked Karin and me if we wanted to go along when she visited the cemeteries.

"Sure, " Karin answered.

"No, I don't want to go this time, but I'll go after you know which spot it will be," I replied. I had been to a lot of cemeteries last summer when Mom was working on her genealogy book. I remembered how hot and tired I'd gotten after walking around looking for someone's grave when we didn't even know exactly where it was supposed to be. No, I wasn't willing to wander around a cemetery again so soon.

Dad and Mom agreed on a plot at Santa Barbara Cemetery. Grandma and Grandpa bought the one right next to it.

"Why didn't you buy a place for us too?" Karin asked when she found out about it.

I wondered why too. After all, we would die some day and need a gravesite. Mom said that when we died we would probably be much older and would want to be buried with our husbands. I guess that made sense.

It was getting more and more difficult to get Dad in and out of bed. He was very weak and Mom had to pull him into a sitting position and someone else had to help support his back. Helping him down the stairs for the day was becoming almost impossible. Sometimes I would help by moving his feet from step to step.

Dad wanted us to get him a hospital bed so he would be more comfortable. We rented one and put it in the family room. He liked it because the head was adjustable and he could watch TV and enjoy the fireplace. Mom even had an extension phone installed so he could talk to friends without going upstairs.

The next weekend was Easter and we joined the Crabbs and Bennetts at Don and Shirely Gesink's house for dinner. I remember that Dad had a terrible time sitting up straight to eat. Everyone was trying to help by positioning pillows around him. Dad was kind of like he had been on the snow trip—very quiet with a strange stare on his face. He was having a lot of trouble with eating now because he was losing control of his hands. Sometimes he would have his hand in his food and not even know it. I felt very sorry for him because I knew he couldn't help it.

"Mom, do you think Dad could come to see my dance tonight?" I asked on Tuesday. I was doing a dance for our school talent show and of course I wanted Mom and Dad to come.

"I'll ask him, honey."

Dad agreed to come so Mom and Judy brought him in his wheelchair, and it really meant a lot to me. They had to leave shortly after my dance because Dad was getting thinner now and was uncomfortable when he sat too long at a time. The night he came to watch my dance was the last time my dad ever left the house.

On Wednesday evening Dr. Henderson came to the house to check on Dad.

"Hi girls," he said as he passed us in the entry way.

He didn't stay very long and didn't even examine Dad, only asked him questions. Mom was right! The doctor could do nothing more to help him. The only thing they could do was help ease the pain and make him as comfortable as possible. The nurse would show Mom how to give him shots when the pain pills were no longer strong enough to help.

"What are you doing?" I asked Mom the next afternoon as she fiddled with a needle and an orange.

"This is how the nurse said I should practice giving shots," she replied.

"Oh," I commented as I turned to go outside. I couldn't believe that all of this was really happening. 'Oh God, please make this all just a bad dream,' I said silently to myself. And yet deep down inside I could no longer deny the facts.

Later that day my friend Allyn started bragging to me about how she had known more about my dad's illness than I did. I ran home crying and told Mom what she had said.

"I've always told you and Karin the truth about Dad. Even Dr. Henderson talked to you," she said. "Maybe Allyn thinks you don't realize Dad is dying because you never talk about it to your friends."

She was right of course. I guess I had been trying to ignore the whole situation, hoping it would all go away.

Mom gave me some books to read about dying. It helped to read about other kids' experiences during and after a death in their family. It still didn't seem possible that all of this was happening to my family.

Either Mom or Grandma would sleep on the sofa in the family room at night now. They wanted to be near Dad when he needed help during the night. He would wake up because he needed to go to the bathroom, and Grandma had brought a bell for Dad to ring when he woke up. But, by the time someone went to help him it was too late. His brain was playing tricks on him and he was losing control of his bladder. The doctor had suggested that Mom get a catheter to put on Dad. This is a tube with a plastic bag at the end to collect urine. Then Dad would not have to worry about accidents and we wouldn't always have to be changing the sheets. It was very painful for him when he had to be moved around in bed.

Grandma was a retired nurse and she helped take good care of Dad. She would give him bed baths and straighten up his bed. Mom would help him eat and give him his medicine, and she spent a lot of time just talking with him.

Friday I happened to come into the family room and saw that Mom and Dad were both crying as Katie lay beside Dad. That night Mom told us that it didn't look like Dad would be with us very much longer.

A Visit to the Cemetery

THE NEXT MORNING Mom called Karin and me into her room.

"Girls, I have to go out for a while this morning, but when I return I want you to go somewhere with me. Okay?"

"Sure Mom", we replied.

"Can we play a little while you're gone?"

"Yes, that's fine."

It was the first day of our spring break at school and we were eager to play with our friends, especially if we would have to be gone part of the day. Later as we drove along, Mom began to speak to us.

"Girls you both have seen how Daddy's gotten steadily worse. He is dying. We don't know exactly when the time will come. It could be hours, days or weeks. When the time does come however, a lot of things will happen that I want you to know about."

"Where are we going?" I asked as she turned on to the freeway.

"Well, first of all I want to show you the cemetery. Is that all right with you?"

We nodded silently.

Santa Barbara Cemetery is a beautiful place. It is right next to the ocean and Dad's gravesite was at the top of a hill surrounded by a lot of old graves with fancy monuments. There were lots of trees and you could see sailboats off in the distance. We walked around looking at markers and reading the inscriptions.

"Look at all the pretty flowers," Karin said as she walked toward a new grave. Actually they were starting to dry up, but they were still pretty.

"What's that for?" I asked pointing to a tent on the lawn down at the other end of this section. Mom said that it was a newly dug grave for someone that had just died, but had not yet been buried. A cemetery is a very interesting place.

There were several small buildings that were called mausoleums and we wanted to go look at them. These were graves above ground. They had big drawers that the caskets were placed into and then they were sealed up. These old ones were usually for a family of six to eight people.

"Oh, poor little babies," Karin said sadly as she gazed at some tiny graves. There were a lot of graves for babies and children and we wondered why.

Mom told us that years ago children used to die from diseases that we get immunizations for today. Things like smallpox, measles, diptheria, whooping cough and polio once killed thousands of children each year—many of them before they were even old enough to walk.

An older lady had been walking up and down the rows of markers ever since we arrived, obviously looking for a particular grave since she had flowers in her hand.

"Why don't we offer to help her?" Mom suggested as we walked in her direction. We soon helped her find the right one. She thanked us for our help and as we turned to walk away, I glanced back to watch as she placed her flowers in the cup. One day soon we would be bringing flowers to our dad's grave.

As we drove toward the exit, we circled through the cemetery and Mom showed us the other plot that they had considered. We agreed that the one she and Dad had selected was the very best spot for him.

Next we drove out to the funeral home that Dad would be taken to after he died. We looked around at the chapel where they would put his casket. The lid would be open so people could come to pay their final respects. There would be lots of flowers too, and everyone who came would sign their name in a special book that we would get to keep. The people at the funeral home would make sure that the newspapers were notified of Dad's death and an announcement would be printed stating the information about the funeral service.

As Mom continued to tell us about the events that would occur, we learned that two limousines would come to our house and take us to the funeral. The service would be held at our church. Mom said she and Mrs. Thornton (who is the choir director) had been working on the service for several weeks. She wanted it to be very meaningful to Christians and also a witness to the non-Christians attending. She told us that the casket would be closed at the church service and that the choir would be singing several songs. The congregation would also join in singing special hymns and the pastor would talk about Dad's life and say some prayers.

She also told us that George Ritter was going to take some pictures at the funeral home, church and cemetery; and Dave Thornton would record the service. Mom thought it would be nice to have the tape and pictures to share later—especially for Katie, since she was so young.

"Are we going anywhere else?" I asked as we passed our normal turnoff.

"Just one more stop and then we're done."

A few minutes later we parked in front of a florist shop. We went inside to look at their books of flower arrangements.

"Remember what I told you about the casket? Well, it usually has a large floral arrangement on the top of it that is purchased by the family. I thought you girls might want to pick out the flowers."

"Oh boy!" Karin said excitedly as I began to flip through the many pages.

Karin and I finally decided on yellow roses for Dad. I was glad that Mom was letting us be involved in the plans she had to make.

Dad was really having difficulty eating now, even swallowing his medication. Mom would usually feed him what little bit he would eat. He was definitely getting weaker and never got out of bed at all now. Even though I didn't want to believe it—I could not deny that MY DAD didn't have much longer to live.

On Sunday morning Mom tried to help Dad out of bed because he wanted to go to church. Although he had dropped out of choir long ago, he had continued to attend worship services. Last Sunday was the first time it had been necessary to take him in his wheelchair. It was very important to Dad to live as normal a life as possible for as long as possible, and he wanted to remain close to the church to the end.

"Would it be all right if you didn't go to church today, Den?" Mom asked him as she tried to help him sit up.

He agreed that he was just too tired and weak to get out of bed and told Mom to go ahead without him. Grandma stayed home with him.

Mom was still singing in the choir and they did a special number about God giving us more grace as the burdens grow greater. I could see that Mom was trying not to cry, but she finally had to stop singing during the last verse because tears were rolling down her cheeks. Other people in the choir had tears in their eyes too.

That Sunday afternoon Dad slipped into a semi-coma. He could no longer swallow his pills so Mom started giving him injections. He still said a few words now and then to her, but he was very distant. Mom and Grandma would turn him over in his bed fairly often because he was starting to get sores on his skin from lying in bed so long. Grandpa had gone home on Saturday since there really wasn't anything he could do to help his son. I guess maybe going back to work would help ease the heartache for him.

Since we didn't have school on Monday, we were home when Mrs. Thornton stopped by. It was April 3rd, Grandma's birthday, so Mrs. Thornton had brought her a plant. Mom wasn't home at the time because she had gone to run some errands.

"Where are you going, Mom?" I had asked her earlier as she carried Dad's brown suit down the stairs.

"I have to run some errands and drop this suit by the cleaners," she'd replied. What a weird day. People coming and going. It sure didn't seem much like Grandma's birthday.

Karin got invited to spend the night with the DeBlauws and Mom said that would be fine. They have three girls and had invited Karin and me over to play often during these past months. We always had a good time there.

Dad hadn't said much all day, and by the time I went to bed he was running a high fever. Mom and Grandma got some aspirin down him and sponged him off with cold wash cloths, but Mom hinted to me that he might not make it through the night.

I was almost afraid to come downstairs in the morning, but I soon learned that Dad was still with us. After breakfast I stood by his bed for a minute and then went outside to play with my friends.

Later in the morning Mrs. Vandebeek, who is a nurse and also a friend from church, came by to keep Mom company and help out in any way she could. She was still there at 1:20 in the afternoon when my dad died. Mom called me in and Mrs. Vandebeek drove over to get Karin. We both went downstairs to the family room to see Dad. He looked real white and completely still.

"Why does he look so white and feel so cold?" Karin asked as she reached out and touched Dad's arm.

With tear-swollen eyes Mom explained to us about how the blood circulating through our bodies gives our skin its glow and warmth. Now Dad's heart had stopped and was no longer pumping blood through his body. It's hard to believe that his forehead could have burned so much with fever only last night and now be so cold.

Very soon a lot of friends began to come by the house. They looked in on Dad and hugged Mom, Grandma and Judy. Most of them were either crying or had tears forming in their eyes. Mom had talked to Dr. Henderson, and Mrs. Vandebeek made several calls to people including the funeral home. They would probably be there within the hour to remove Dad's body.

Karin and I went outside to talk to our friends— it seemed like the only thing to do. Katie was not at home because Mrs. Thornton had picked her up earlier in the morning to spend some time playing with her daughter Jodie. As we walked outside Karin started to cry.

"I wish Dad had been able to see the cake we made him last night," she muttered. "It was a special GET WELL CAKE that Janie and I baked and decorated."

We were standing out front when a white panel truck from the mortuary pulled into our driveway. They had come to take our dad from home for the last time. They wrapped him in a white sheet from head to toe and put him on a stretcher. Then they wheeled him out to the truck where they placed him inside and drove away. I was crying hard inside, but only a few tears rolled down my face. Our neighbor, Mrs. Bishop, told us that Dad was okay because at the very moment that he died, Jesus was right there to take his hand and lead him to heaven.

There really wasn't anything we could do so we stayed outside with our friends talking and standing around. I kept an eye on our house because even though I couldn't bear to be inside just then, I didn't want to miss out on anything that went on.

After a while friends stopped coming over and some men came to pick up the hospital bed and wheelchair. When I did go back home, things looked more normal in our house than they had in a long time. I would miss my dad very much in the months ahead, but already I was getting the feeling that life in our house would continue in much the same way that it always had.

The funeral was planned for Friday at one o'clock. Since Mom had made most of the arrangements during the previous weeks, there were only small details to be taken care of. I was glad that she had lots of time to spend with us.

On Thursday afternoon we went to the funeral home to see Dad in his casket. He lay still and cold in the brown suit that Mom had taken to the cleaners on the day before his death.

"He's not white anymore," Karin whispered as we stood by the casket. Make-up had been lightly applied to his face and hands.

Katie wanted to climb in "the box" and give Dad a hug so Mom let her pat him and this satisfied her. Then she reached for the lid and said, "Let's close it up." We didn't stay very long and, as we left, Karin and I signed the book and Mom wrote Katie's name for her. Mom would return again with some special friends, but this was the last time I saw my dad.

In the paper that evening the following article appeared about Dad in the DEATHS COLUMN. It is called an obituary and is a brief summary of his life.

Dennis Frisbie

Dennis Michael Frisbie, 34, of 1037 St. Mary's Lane, died yesterday at his home of a malignant brain tumor.

Born Oct. 7, 1943, in Los Angeles, he attended high school in Gardena and was a graduate of UCSB as a physical science major. He had been employed by IBM Corp. since 1967.

For several years coach for the Santa Barbara Recreation Department swim team, he was also a certified official who spent many hours as referee of swim meets and water polo for both American Athletic Union and high school functions.

Survivors are his wife, Barbara Francene Garriott Frisbie, whom he married Sept. 11, 1965, in Gardena; three daughters, Kelly Anne, Karin Lynn and Katie Marie Frisbie; his parents, Mr. and Mrs. Dennis Edward Frisbie of Saratoga; and a sister, Judy Frisbie, of Los Angeles.

Services will be tomorrow at 1 p.m. at El Camino Orthodox Presbyterian Church, 7526 Calle Real, where he was a member of the choir. Friends may remember the Dennis M. Frisbie Memorial Organ fund in care of the church.

Visitation will be until 4 p.m. tonight and from 8 a.m. to 11 a.m. tomorrow at Welch-Ryce Associates chapel in Goleta. Interment will be at Santa Barbara Cemetery.

DENNIS FRISBIE
Services Tomorrow

71

The Funeral Service

ON FRIDAY THINGS WENT much as Mom had said they would, only there were a lot of extra people at the house. Many friends and relatives from out of town came by in the morning before the service. Friends from church had provided cinnamon rolls for people to eat, but I think the kids were the only ones who ate any.

Two limousines pulled up in front of our house at about 12:30 to take the family members to the service. They were big black cars with very big back seats. After the adults got inside, Karin and I got in and sat on two little "jump seats" that unfolded and just sort of popped up into position. On the five-mile drive to the church no one said anything except Katie. She was too little to understand what was happening on this day.

When we arrived at church, the car that had brought the casket to the service was parked out front. Mom said it was called a hearse. It looked like an extra-long station wagon to me.

I could see people parking their cars and hurrying into the church. We were supposed to

wait until just before the service started before we took our seats.

The first few rows in the front of the sanctuary were reserved for the family members and pall-bearers (these are the men who carry the casket out to the hearse when the service it over). I knew all six of the men Mom had selected for this task. Two of them were very old friends of the family, two were Dad's co-workers at IBM, and the last two were close friends from church.

While we waited to take our seats, we were given little folders with facts about Dad listed and a program of the service. It would last about an hour.

"Let's go now, girls," Mom said as the usher motioned for us to come. She took Karin and me by the hand and we walked quickly to our seats (Katie was in the nursery with a friend for the service, but she would join us again for the trip to the cemetery). Shortly afterward, the choir began to sing. The service was just like Mom said it would be. We sang several hymns, the pastor prayed and spoke of Dad's life, and the choir sang two more numbers. My favorite one was called "This World Is Not My Home". I was glad that the service was recorded and that we would be able to play it again later.

For the closing number we all stood up to join the choir in the singing of the "Hallelujah Chorus". Then the man from the mortuary thanked everyone for coming and told us there would be a procession to the cemetery and everyone should turn on their car lights to let others know that they were part of a funeral. Then the ushers came forward and row by row dismissed the congregation. We remained seated until the church was empty and then Mom led us outside where we watched the pallbearers load the casket into the back of the hearse.

Grandma had gone immediately to the car and was still crying when we got in. She was very sad. I was sad too, but I didn't cry. Only when our minister had been talking about how Dad spent a lot of time with us camping and traveling did I have to fight back the tears. The rest of the service was very encouraging and almost happy. I guess what we were really doing was rejoicing for Dad because his suffering was over and now he was in heaven and at peace.

Almost everyone from the service went to the cemetery. The gravesite that we had visited less than a week ago looked very different today. The grave had been opened and two silver poles lay across the hole to support the casket. You couldn't see any dirt though, because it had all been covered with artificial grass. A canopy covered the site and flowers were arranged along the backside of the grave. Mom had selected a marker several weeks earlier and the people at the monument place had completed it and it was propped up at

the side. Besides Dad's name and the dates of his birth and death, the following Bible verse was inscribed on it: "O DEATH, WHERE IS THY STING? O GRAVE, WHERE IS THY VICTORY? THANKS BE TO GOD, WHICH GIVETH US VICTORY THROUGH OUR LORD JESUS CHRIST. I COR. 15:55, 57."

After the pallbearers positioned the casket over the grave, our pastor said a few words and offered a prayer. It was over now. Men from the cemetery would lower the casket after we left. Mom had been holding Katie during this short service, but she put her down while talking with some friends. Suddenly Katie dashed towards the grave. Someone whisked her up into their arms just before she reached the casket. The people who had seen her laughed at her surprise of being intercepted. I guess she wanted some of the pretty flowers. The man from the mortuary took several roses from the casket and gave them to Mom.

"I think we should leave now so that the others will feel free to go also," Grandpa said as he put his arm around Mom's shoulder. And so we entered the big black car for the last ride.

When we arrived home, sandwiches and salads were waiting for us. Ruth Lemkuil and Bev Ruiz had returned to the house immediately after the service to organize the food that ladies in the church had prepared for family, friends and out-of-town guests. A lot of people did come back to the house, but no one stayed very long. The past few weeks had been very hard on Mom and I know she looked forward to having our house get back to normal as soon as possible. Grandma and Grandpa Frisbie, Judy, Mana, Joe and Uncle Ronnie all spent the night with us, but they planned to leave in the morning.

After Grandma, Grandpa and Judy left for home, we drove our car to the cemetery while Joe, Mana and Ronnie followed in their car. They would head back to Los Angeles after stopping with us at the cemetery.

The grave looked much different than it had yesterday. All of the dirt was back in place and the lawn had been carefully returned to its position. The marker was cemented directly over the head of the grave and the flowers that had been so fresh yesterday lay wilting on the grass.

"Can we have some flowers?" I asked Mom.

Karin and I took great care selecting just the ones we liked best from the bouquets. Mom took some yellow ribbon from the cascade that we had bought for the casket.

"I think I'll dry some of the yellow roses and put a piece of ribbon with them so you can each have one," she said smiling.

We didn't stay very long. We said good bye to Mana, Joe and Ronnie and returned home to begin a new life for ourselves.

The next few weeks did not seem very different from the times when Dad had been away on business trips. In fact it was hard to believe that he was not just away and would be back at any time. We talked about him a lot.

Karin and I wondered how our lives would change now that we didn't have a father. We asked if we would still get to do the same things we had enjoyed, like camping and traveling.

"Who's going to fix things around the house?" I asked one day when my bike needed some repair.

Fortunately we had many friends and neighbors who would come to our rescue when we couldn't take care of something ourselves.

Karin was afraid that Mom would have to go to work to earn money and that I would be the boss over her when Mom wasn't around. This discussion brought the first real laughter to our dinner table in months. Actually I wouldn't have minded if Mom did have to work, but I was relieved when she told us that because of life insurance, social security and IBM benefits, she would not need to go to work to support us. And yes, we would continue to do most of the things that we enjoyed when Dad was alive.

We would miss Dad VERY MUCH and sometimes cry just thinking about him, but OUR lives would continue.

How do you feel when someone you love very much dies? I guess my sister Karin said it best in this note she wrote for her 1st grade teacher:

Apr 4/today / tuesday

From Karin F.

Dear Mrs. Metcalf how have you been? Did you have a nice Spring? Yes no April 4 MY DaDDy died. it Was Sad But O.K. I Wasn't There When My Dad died but my mom called me home to See him. he Was peaceful and he Didn't have any pain. he didn't Suffer theEnd.

please read to class

1978

79

Yes I'm sad, but I'll be okay. Death has claimed my father, but NO ONE can wipe away the many happy memories of the times we shared.

EPILOGUE

A Mother's Reflections

IT IS HARD TO BELIEVE that ten years have passed since we first heard that awful phrase—"brain tumor". Yet, life does go on for those left behind when a loved one dies. During the past ten years I have often wondered if I did the right thing involving my children in their father's illness, impending death and funeral arrangements. Looking back, I must admit my choices were correct. I am very proud of how Kelly, Karin & Katie are doing in life.

At nineteen, Kelly is a sophomore in college majoring in English and music. She works part time typesetting for the school newspaper and also does office work in the psychology department. She graduated from high school with a 4.0 average and was Valedictorian of her class of over 500 students.

Karin is sixteen and currently a Junior in high school. At her Eighth Grade Graduation she was honored as the Outstanding Girl in her class. Currently she is a Candy Striper at the local hospital, and also works part-time doing clerical work in a local doctor's office. She is considering a career in the medical field.

Katie is now eleven, a good student, musician and athlete. Although she doesn't remember the experiences she was a part of ten years ago, they definitely contributed to the young lady she is today. She was the one who caused me to smile when she spoke confidently to a three-year-old acquaintance, "My Daddy died. He's in the box at the cemetery." She also brought the tears one cool evening as she helped me start a fire by crinkling up newspapers. "My Daddy used to make fires," she said softly.

What was life like for our family during the early days after Dennis' death? We tried to live a normal life. I still sang in the choir and went to Bible studies. The girls were active in church, Scouts and 4H, and Katie started nursery school. I was fortunate that with such young children I did not have to go to work. However, there was such a void in my life that I eventually got involved with a widow's group & Parents Without Partners, started an Amway business, took some classes and did volunteer work.

At first we lived day to day and then week to week. Our social life was centered around a group of close friends from the church who went out of their way to include us in their lives. I'll never forget the camping trip with the Crabbs to nearby

Lake Cachuma. It was such a small thing really, but it showed us that we could still go camping and have fun. Of course the girls had to be more helpful and responsible, but that was good for them.

As the months passed, I kept looking for things to keep me busy. Doing some painting and redecorating seemed to help. The girls had fun pulling off wallpaper and helping select new furniture, fabrics and colors. I think somehow we made our first Christmas alone a little easier to bear because the house had been redecorated. Again, we sent a Christmas letter and picture to our friends and relatives:

Christmas 1978

"FOR GOD SO LOVED THE WORLD, THAT HE GAVE HIS ONLY BEGOTTEN SON, THAT WHOEVER BELIEVES IN HIM SHOULD NOT PERISH, BUT HAVE ETERNAL LIFE" John 3:16

Dear Friends and Relatives,

It's hard to believe that a whole year has passed and soon we will be celebrating Christmas once again. It has been a year of great loss and sorrow for our family, but nevertheless it has been full of blessings too.

Den has been gone for eight months now and we have learned that time has a wonderful way of healing our wounds. The hurt is still there, but the tears come less often now and laughter frequently fills our home as we remember the happy times we had with "Daddy". We are indeed thankful for the many precious memories that remain with us.

The girls have brought laughter and joy to my life in ways that only children can. What a blessing they have been—if only because they keep me

so busy! I'm truly fortunate to be able to remain at home with them during these formative years. What "Little Women" they are becoming.

We all have adopted a positive approach to our new life-style and work together to continue to do our favorite things. We are confident that the Lord will continue to answer our prayers and provide for our needs throughout the new year.

We wish you all a Merry Christmas and a New Year full of blessings.

Love to all,

Barbara, Kelly, Karin and Katie

Grandma and Grandpa Frisbie celebrated the holidays with us and, considering the circumstances, it was a very nice Christmas.

Time passed and although I was very busy, I was lonely. I wanted someone to go to dinner with occasionally and Karin wanted a "new daddy". We talked about this possibility, but there just didn't seem to be any "appropriate" single men available. Our friends were very protective of us and they didn't want me to date "just anybody". I went to a Christian singles conference in February of 1979. It was one of the first times I'd been able to get away and it was an enjoyable experience. I met people from all over California and we shared about our lives as single parents. I thought I would like to attend another retreat sometime.

The girls wanted to go on a vacation, but I was leery of undertaking anything like we had done in the past. After all, it would not be easy for a woman and three young girls to travel alone. We came up with a wonderful idea. We would invite my mother to join us for a trip around the country on the train. Then, we could get off and visit relatives and see many historic places. It was an experience we will never forget. From Los Angeles to New Orleans, Atlanta to Philadelphia, Chicago to Seattle and back to Santa Barbara; we saw Amtrak at its best, and worst. We visited an old plantation and a modern-day farm. We rode in a horse-drawn carriage and touched the Liberty Bell. We laughed when Mom didn't get off the train in Jamestown, North Dakota and the conductor had to hold the train while I searched for her. We found her in the dining car about to have some breakfast. After three weeks we returned home somewhat weary, but we had become seasoned travelers who were not afraid to venture out on our own.

In September, 1979, I attended another Christain singles retreat in Northern California. I didn't know it then, but this retreat was to change our lives. It was there that I met John Juneau, a widower with three young daughters. We shared our experiences one afternoon sitting on the lawn in front of the conference center. I learned that he had attended college in Santa Barbara and that we knew some of the same people. We laughed and talked and then went our separate ways—or so I thought.

The holidays came and went. This Christmas was somehow harder than the previous year.

Maybe it was because I was beginning to think that we would never have a complete family again. The usual picture and card was sent out and this time I was in the picture too.

CHRISTMAS 1979

To every thing there is a season, and a time to every purpose under the heaven: A time to be born, and a time to die . . . A time to weep, and a time to laugh; A time to mourn, and a time to dance . . . Eccl. 3:1-4

Dear Friends and Relatives,

We send you greetings and a wish that your holiday season be filled with peace and joy!

As I ponder where the year went I am filled with mixed emotions. The early months brought holidays and special dates that reminded us of Dennis' absence. When April 4th arrived I felt that a milestone had been reached—the first year was over without any major difficulties. The month of June was highlighted by a beautiful Organ Dedication Ceremony. We praise God for the generous gifts of family and friends that made this memorial a reality. It was indeed a very fitting close to a special chapter in our lives.

With summer approaching we began making plans for our first vacation alone. As some of you know, we embarked on a three-week train trip around the country that proved to be quite an adventure. Accompanied by my mom, the girls and I visited such places as New Orleans, Georgia, North Carolina, Philadelphia, North Dakota and

Seattle. Despite the lack of air-conditioning, late trains, lost luggage and even a bus that ran out of gas; we look back on the trip with fond memories of the time spent with loved ones far away. And of course we laughingly tell ourselves that without the problems, the trip would have been just another "ordinary" vacation. I guess it was just the experience we needed to prove to ourselves that we could handle almost any situation if we put our minds to it. Therefore, be aware that the Frisbie family plans to continue its travels and you will be forewarned when we are headed in your direction.

As summer came to an end activities seemed to spring up from nowhere. In addition to all the

school-related functions, the older girls continue
with piano lessons (Ugh!), 4-H and Pioneer Girls.
Kelly is also playing the flute and Karin is learn-
ing how to play a soprano-recorder. Katie is attending pre-school four mornings a week this year
so I thought I would have a lot of time to myself.
SURPRISE!!!

One morning is devoted to a writing class (I'm
going to finish my book yet), another to the Santa
Barbara Historical Society (the training program
for their guides is both educational and enjoyable); and with the other two mornings I have been
developing an Amway Distributorship. The latter
I decided to try for the fun of it and also as a means
of motivating me to get out a little more. I'm happy
to say that the business is both fun and profitable.
I'm looking forward to attending a seminar at the
Disneyland Hotel in January which should come
at just about the right time to lift me out of the post-
holiday doldrums.

By the way, did you notice the new addition to
our family this year? Her name is Terry and she is
a 4-month old "Humane Society Special". After all
these years of postponing the inevitability of acquiring a dog—I finally ran out of excuses. Of
course my last remark as we piled into the car was
"OK, we can get a dog, but NOT a puppy who
chews up everything and isn't house-broken." So
much for last words.

Love to all,

Barbara, Kelly, Karin and Katie

In January I received an unexpected call from
John whom I had met at the retreat in September.

He lived in Grass Valley, California about 450 miles to the north of Santa Barbara in the Sierra Nevada Foothills. John was going to be in the Santa Barbara area in February and wanted to meet us for lunch. Well, that one lunch led to many more conversations and meetings and on July 12, 1980 we were married in Santa Barbara in a traditional ceremony. I was pleased and honored to be escorted down the aisle by Grandpa Frisbie and the girls were all bridesmaids. They referred to it as "OUR WEDDING". The Frisbie family moved to the Grass Valley area and a new family was born.

The move from Santa Barbara, combined with acquiring three new sisters and a step-father over-night, had a traumatic affect on the girls, especially Kelly at age twelve. The first year was not an easy one for any of us. Christmas Day found Kelly and me in tears—partly because for the first time in thirteen years Grandma and Grandpa Frisbie could not be with us for the holidays, and also because things were just different. Our new family was struggling to make its own traditions. Eventually things would settle into a combination of both Juneau and Frisbie holiday traditions, but never again would things be like they had in the past. One Frisbie tradition we kept was the annual Christmas letter and picture, which appropriately in 1980, was a wedding picture.

O SING TO THE LORD A NEW SONG, FOR HE HAS DONE MARVELOUS THINGS. Psalm 98:1

Christmas 1980

Dear Friends and Relatives,

The Lord has truly done marvelous things in our lives during this past year. And, as we celebrate His birth, we extend greetings and best wishes for a happy holiday season to all of you from our newly created family.

The seed that sprouted into our family of eight was first planted in September, 1979. It was then that a widow with three daughters talked briefly with a widower (who also happened to have three girls) one afternoon at a Christian Singles Conference at Mt. Hermon. At this time there was no indication that even a friendship might develop between us. After all, with John living in Grass Valley, and Santa Barbara some 450 miles away, there was little likelihood of future communication between us. However, someone greater than us was definitely in control of the situation and with the new year came a series of phone calls, letters and visits that eventually led to our marriage on July 12th.

Blending our two families into one has been a major undertaking. In our case, the sum of one plus one equaled eight. We have all had adjustments to make over the past months and as we all grow in our relationships with the others we have experienced joy and sorrow, fun and frustrations. One thing for certain is that there is never a dull moment around our house. We are pleased to report that for the most part the girls have adjusted nicely to each other and are beginning to act more like sisters every day. The girls have even discovered the fun of having so many sisters that if one is angry with you, it really doesn't matter because there are four others to play with you.

Some of you have had a chance to meet the new family members and yet many have not. It seems appropriate therefore to make a few introductions.

Katie Frisbie (4 1/2) - the "baby" of the family, she is very active and sometimes a nuisance as far as her big sisters are concerned. However, they do enjoy spoiling her somewhat since she is often irresistible.

Cindy Juneau (7) - a 2nd grader this year, she seems to be enjoying all the activities at school. Her favorite hobbies are skating and riding her bike.

Karin Frisbie (9 1/2) - in the 4th grade, she has adjusted very well to her new school. It was not easy to leave her many friends in Santa Barbara, but she enjoys "playing school" with her built-in playmates and helping Mom in the kitchen.

Christy Juneau (10) - a 5th grader, she is probably our quietest daughter. She enjoys reading, playing the piano and wants to learn to sew as soon as Mom finds some time to teach her.

Carol Juneau (12) - a 7th grader, Carol enjoys most sports and was on the school volleyball team this fall. We often see Carol with a book in her hand, since reading is also a favorite pastime.

Kelly Frisbie (12 1/2) - in the 7th grade also, she spends a lot of time at the piano or in the kitchen baking. Like Karin, Kelly misses her old friends, but has begun to make new ones and there have even been some indications that she likes it here in Nevada City.

As for myself, I love it here in the Sierra Foothills. Right now we are at about the 2700' elevation and I am really enjoying the change of seasons. The crisp, cold air during the fall is invigorating and the spectacular colors of the trees last month was nature's finest showing. John has been busy splitting wood and we spend most evenings enjoying the warmth of a fire in our wood burning stove.

We are looking toward our first snowfall of the year. If things go as planned, next year we will be building a new home up at the 3800' level. At that elevation we should have no problem getting an ample supply of the white stuff.

John, a former school teacher, is now in the real estate and development field. Right now his office is busy with a 44-unit condominium project.

He is also studying for his broker's license and that involves classes two nights per week. At times I'm sure he must feel terribly out-numbered by the "7 Women" in his house, but fortunately he has a good sense of humor (even our three dogs are females).

Naturally we would love to see you all. Please accept our invitation to visit us whenever you are in the area. We probably won't be travelling any great distances next summer because of the construction of our house, but perhaps the following year we will be able to make one big circle around the country. John and I are both anxious to "show-off" our new family.

It is always good to reflect on the past and consider the many blessings we have received. We are indeed thankful for all that God has accomplished in our lives this year. He has done marvelous things and continues to work wonders in our lives. We pray that all is well with each of you and extend our heartiest wish for a very MERRY CHRISTMAS and a BLESSED NEW YEAR.

Love to all,

John, Barbara, Kelly, Carol, Christy
Karin, Cindy, Katie

I am pleased that after seven years the Juneau/Frisbie family has evolved into a close, loving family. The girls all get along beautifully, sharing clothes, rooms and "girl talk". Of course there is some occasional sibling rivalry but it has never been a major problem. No one ever stays mad for very long.

94

I believe that the experiences relating to illness and death have made our girls stronger and better able to withstand the everyday pressures of life. They know that "life is not fair" and that you learn to adapt and persevere. I was so proud of all six of them last year when my mother was diagnosed with lung cancer. Near the end of her life she moved in with us and the girls spent time in her room doing their homework, watching TV or just visiting with her. They were attentive to her needs—getting her food and drink, helping her to the bathroom, giving her medicine. They knew she was dying, but they were not afraid. They cared about "Mana" and wanted to be helpful. They were saddened on the morning of September 20, 1986, when she passed away quietly in her sleep at our home; but I think they felt good within themselves, knowing that they had helped to make her last months happy and comfortable.

Had I done the right thing ten years ago exposing my young daughters to the world of pain, suffering and death? Yes, I think so. Don't be afraid to talk to your children, to explain, to comfort and even to cry with them. They will be better people because of the experiences they share with you during a time of illness and death. I know my girls are. In fact, because of our family's previous experiences with death and our strong Christian faith, Kelly and Karin were able to take part in Mom's funeral by singing a song whose message brought comfort and hope to those attending:

In His Love by Ed DeGarmo and Dana Key

In His love there's a place where you can always
    hide away.
In His love there's no need to run, no need to be
    afraid.
If the world's a sea of trouble, you can always rise
    above,
If you know that you are safely in His love.

In His love where all pain and sorrow quickly fade
    away,
In His love there's a bright tomorrow just beyond
    today.
If your heart is filled with sorrow, if it's all you can
    think of,
Still there'll be a new tomorrow in His love.
His love is never far away, yet sometimes hard to
    see.
If we would take the time to pray, His love would
    flow through you and me.

In His love there's a place where you can watch the
    world go by.
In His love there's no need to hurry; ev'rything's
    on time.
When the world's a sea of trouble, you can always
    rise above,
If you know that you are safely in His love.

Oh, in His love there's a place where you can
    always hide away.
In His love there's no need to run, no need to be
    afraid.
If your heart is filled with sorrow, if it's all you can
    think of,
Still there'll be a new tomorrow in His love.

If you have or are about to experience a death in your family or that of someone close to you, I hope the message in this book has been meaningful to you. Take heart in the following words of the little girl who ten years ago at age six could so innocently express the feeling that her daddy's death was sad, but OK. Now at sixteen she writes:

Recalling the death of my dad brings both happy and, of course, sad memories. I was faced with a major tragedy that affected the outcome of my "younger years" and continues to have an impact on my life today.

I can clearly recall the day that my dad died. The night before I had slept over at Janie DeBlauw's house. We had had a good time playing, but we also talked about Dad and his illness. We decided to bake him a get well cake. We were so proud of our cake and very excited about giving it to him. However, before we could take it over to him, Mrs. DeBlauw received a phone call. After hanging up the phone she walked over to me and picked me up in her arms, and began to explain the situation that I would encounter when I arrived home in a few minutes. My dad was dead! My first reaction was, "this is unreal, I don't believe it!. He couldn't just die without saying goodbye . . . and especially without getting his cake!"

During the past couple of months I realized that Dad was often very sick, but I never really believed that he would die. "Daddy is dying" were just words Mom used—they had no real meaning for a six year old. Surely he would get well soon. But no, when I arrived home I learned that what I was told was true. I went down to Dad's bed and held his hand—it was so cold and he looked so still and peaceful. I wanted him to talk and laugh with me again, but he made no sounds nor made any movements. After a few minutes I was forced to leave because the men from the funeral home would soon be there to take him away. I ran off to tell the neighbors.

Of course they didn't believe a six year old, so they came to check it out for themselves. There were people coming and going constantly and Mom was busy taking care of all the necessary business. It was nice to have friends and relatives comfort us at this time. Later that day I wrote a letter to my kindergarten teacher which I took to class the next Monday since my dad died during Easter Vacation.

I can remember crying myself to sleep the first few nights, just wishing that he'd come back. I was the curious type and always liked to talk about Dad and know everything that was going on. We visited Dad at the funeral home and in a few days the time for the funeral arrived. We climbed into a black car and went to the church. I don't remember the service very clearly, I just remember everyone crying a lot.

On Monday my teacher read the letter out loud to the class. It didn't bother me because what it said was true and I wanted people to know that my dad had died. I didn't want to tell friends individually because I thought that they would just think I wanted attention and sympathy. Besides, I was afraid that I might start crying. The class was all very understanding and comforting.

The next months were very challenging and hard for me. Sometimes I felt deprived and kept wondering, why me? I was very close to my dad and I missed him very much. I liked it when Mom reminded me that of all us girls, I resembled Dad the most. It made me feel special. Since I missed Dad and the things we used to do together, I often asked Mom about getting a new daddy. I didn't know then that in two years time a new dad would be part of the picture.

I am very satisfied with the way Mom handled things and now as I look back, I wonder how she ever managed everything. We, the kids, were always kept informed and were made not to feel left out. We visited the gravesite, had talks with the doctor and also with Mom. From the very beginning I think Mom knew what the outcome was going to be and yet she was strong for us. I wouldn't have wanted anything done differently— except for him not dying at all.

I feel that in general this experience has helped me grow and made me a stronger person. I've been exposed to death and can relate to others that may have had a similar experience. I can comfort them because I have actually experienced it myself. On the other hand, I feel somewhat deprived of what I thought was a perfect life and am often jealous of those who still live with their natural parents. In spite of it all, I have come to realize that Dad died for a reason. I have faith that God will continue to use this experience to my advantage, and help me to be a person that my dad would be proud to call his daughter.